GET Set

A Spiritual Preparation for
Short-term Missions Partners

By
Melissa Heiland

ISBN: 978-0-9767645-5-7

Published by IMB, Richmond, Virginia

Dewey Decimal Classification: 266
Subject Heading: MISSIONS

Unless otherwise noted, all Scripture quotations are taken from the Holman Christian Standard Bible®, Copyright © 1999, 2000, 2002, 2003 by Holman Bible Publishers. Used by permission. Holman Christian Standard Bible®, Holman CSB® and HCSB® are federally registered trademarks of Holman Bible Publishers.

Photos in the printed work are not representational of actual story content. Source of photos is the International Mission Board.

Cover and interior design: Natasha C. Fullard

Editor: Kim P. Davis, Richmond, VA

To my Lord and Savior Jesus Christ

and

to my husband, Ken,

who will always be my hero

and the wind beneath my wings

ACKNOWLEDGMENTS

I owe a debt of gratitude to the IMB, which introduced me to mission work, trained me to be a missionary and put a great deal of effort into this book.

I would like to thank all of the volunteer short-term missions partners who have served our Lord with us around the world.

I would also like to thank my children: Michael, our oldest son, who has traveled with me around the world and has dedicated his life to serving the Lord as a missionary doctor; Joshua, who was the first to know about this book and believe in me and who is bravely serving our country in the United States Air Force; and Meli, our only daughter, who spent many hours typing this manuscript. Jack, Andy and Nick, our adventures together have just begun.

I would like to thank my parents, Pat and Jim Gainey, whose loving care of our children makes our mission trips possible.

And finally, thanks go to my Christian sisters (you know who you are) who faithfully lift me up in prayer.

INTRODUCTION

I am so excited that you have answered God's call to participate in a mission trip! I know you will be blessed beyond your wildest dreams. I hope this little book will help prepare you spiritually to do the work God has called you to do.

Each day of this 31-day journey, Scripture and some related thoughts are provided for you. Read the Scripture, enjoy the story, pray and write down in a journal what you believe God is saying to you. I'm sure you will be blessed by spending this special time with the Lord.

God's Word has the answer for any of your concerns as you anticipate your adventure. You are not alone. Other short-term partners can relate to your feelings of anxiety, excitement, doubt and gratitude. You will have your own stories to tell about your upcoming experience, and God will use you to bless others with what He has taught you. Run the race!

See you in heaven, if not before!

Blessings and love,
Melissa Heiland
Beautiful Feet International and Short-term Missions Partner

Day One:

Facing a Giant

Read 1 Samuel 17:32-51

"But Saul replied, 'You can't go fight this Philistine. You're just a youth, and he's been a warrior since he was young.'" (1 Samuel 17:33)

Finally reaching the Guatemalan village at an altitude of 10,000 feet, Cathy was overwhelmed at the many cases of tuberculosis, conjunctivitis, urinary tract infections and scabies. People came from everywhere to see a doctor. While Cathy was way out of her comfort zone as a participant on this mission trip, she learned what it meant to take up Jesus' cross and follow Him. While the team prayed on the last night in the village, Cathy couldn't help but think that she could never go on another mission trip. Missions was too scary. However, she felt like the Lord was saying, "Don't you think that I faced fear when I walked up that hill with a tree on my back?" It wasn't a reprimand but a gentle question.

Many times, as we seek to serve the Lord, we feel like we are facing a giant. The giant may surface as criticism, discouragement, fear, lack of funds or many other things. We feel like the problem is too big for us to handle, and the truth is that it often is. Praise God that He included the story of David and Goliath in His love letter for us! "David said to the Philistine, 'You come against me with a dagger, spear, and sword, but I come against you in the name of the LORD of Hosts.'" (1 Samuel 17:45a)

Lord, I thank You for who You are. I thank You that You can slay my giant. As I seek to serve You, help me to be courageous as I trust in You.

Amen.

Day Two:

Armor of God

Read Ephesians 6:10-18

"Finally, be strengthened by the Lord and by His vast strength. Put on the full armor of God so that you can stand against the tactics of the Devil."
(Ephesians 6:10-11)

"Who am I to lead a short-term team to South Africa?" Kimberly questioned God as she had real doubts that she could effectively be a leader. She had the desire to go, but gnawing thoughts of not being good enough to lead or minister kept defeating her. It wasn't until she shared her fears with an older, godly woman that she was confronted with the truth—Satan was doing his best to discourage her and change her mind about going. With new determination and a prayerful attitude, Kimberly gave her fears over to the Lord.

Often we feel like life is a battle because it is! We are involved in a spiritual battle—a battle that has already been won! The devil is scheming against us, especially if we are undertaking big things for God. God has provided everything we need to take our stand against the enemy. We are vulnerable without our armor. Let us remember every day to put on each piece of armor: truth, righteousness, peace, faith, salvation and the Word of the Spirit.

Father, we go in Your name, the name above all names. We thank You that You have not left us vulnerable but strong in You and Your power. Thank You for the perfect armor that You have provided for us. Please help us to remember to put it on each day. *We pray in Jesus' name. Amen.*

CLEAN HEART

Read Psalm 51

"Purify me with hyssop, and I will be clean; wash me, and I will be whiter than snow." (Psalm 51:7)

When Gary, a missionary, and his son arrived with friends at one of their favorite camping spots in Guatemala, they were shocked to discover that the campsites had been poorly maintained, unlike years before. Weeds, briars, bushes and soupy mud covered the area that used to be picturesque beside the now inaccessible lake. Nevertheless, they cleaned up the site the best they could and pitched their tents. After preparing shelter, the fathers and sons took rods and reels down to the lake. When the rain started, it wasn't long before their shoes stuck in the mire, and briars tore at their clothing and exposed skin. Most of the group went back to the campsite, but two of the boys stayed to fish longer in the dark. When the boys didn't return, the fathers searched for their sons. Finally, they were found wandering in the mud and briars, lost and miserable.

How many times have we chosen to stay behind in the darkness and then lost the trail back home, wandering in the mud and briars of sin? So often I identify with the psalmist as he writes, "My sin is always before me." I want to go and preach the Good News to the poor and broken in spirit, but I know that first I must confess my sins to the Lord. God delights in cleansing our hearts so that He can use us for His kingdom. His Word tells us that He will give us clean hearts so that we can teach transgressors His ways and bring them to Him. Take time to confess your sins to the One who is faithful and just to forgive and cleanse you from all unrighteousness.

Heavenly Father, I come to You now as a sinner, seeking Your mercy and Your forgiveness. Cleanse me, Father, as I prepare to go and spread Your Good News. I pray that sinners will turn to You. *I pray in Jesus' name. Amen.*

Day Four:

Becoming a Slave

Read 1 Corinthians 9:19-23

"For although I am free from all people, I have made myself a slave to all, in order to win more people." *(1 Corinthians 9:19)*

When we entered the restaurant in Southeast Asia, we were horrified to see what looked like an aquarium in the entryway. It was not filled with fish but with hundreds of crawling scorpions. Soon our fears were confirmed—these creatures were to be a part of our dinner. The waitress scooped the writhing animals from the tank and took them to the back to be prepared for our consumption. With deep breaths and heart-felt prayers, we chewed and swallowed these crunchy creatures. Honestly, they tasted like bacon!

As a missionary, Paul says in 1 Corinthians 9 that he makes himself a slave to everyone. What does this mean to us? It means that we serve others, no matter our limitations. It means that if we minister in a culture where women and men eat in separate rooms, we eat in separate rooms as we seek to witness and build relationships. We may need to change the way we dress, what we eat or how we greet each other. We may need to learn a new language or eat with our hands. We submit ourselves to the people we are trying to turn to Christ. What a privilege this is! Our citizenship is, after all, in heaven.

Lord, as I submit to You, help me to submit to others. I pray for the salvation of many as we go to do Your work. Use me and teach me.
In Jesus' name. Amen.

DAY FIVE:

GOD'S POWER

Read Psalm 77

*"You are the God who works wonders; You revealed
Your strength among the peoples." (Psalm 77:14)*

Before John ever left his home country to travel to São Paulo, Brazil, his
faith was stretched. Visa problems delayed his departure, and he was unable
to leave with the rest of the mission team. Two days later, he finally made it,
having to find the hotel by taxi on his own. Once he arrived, he didn't waste
any time. During that week, John shared Christ with a bedridden man, his
wife and granddaughter. All three came to Christ. Another family, grieving
over the death of a loved one, wanted to talk to John. Because John's brother
had recently died, they shared a common grief. As he talked with them,
he told them about the Comforter who loves them. Five in this family also
received God's grace. God brought His message and displayed His power to
hurting people through His servant who struggled to get a visa.

Let us never forget that we serve a God of miracles. As you prepare to go
on your missions journey, go expectantly. Expect God to display His power
among the peoples. Look for God in your life, in the lives of your team
members and in the lives of the people you are going to serve. Does raising
support seem impossible? Is getting a visa difficult? Do the hearts of the
people seem hard? Are you facing health problems? Look to God who parted
the Red Sea!

Father, I know You are a God who performs miracles. I ask You to
display Your power among the people. Show Your power here and now as my
team prepares to go. Provide all that we need so that we can serve You. And
Father, do a miracle in the lives of the people we are going to serve. Redeem
Your people. We praise You for what You will do in and through us.
In Jesus' name. Amen.

THE SPIRIT'S POWER

Read 1 Corinthians 2:1-5

"My speech and my proclamation were not with persuasive words of wisdom, but with a demonstration of the Spirit and power." (1 Corinthians 2:4)

Three women from South Carolina totally surprised a young, new worker serving in East Asia. For a year, she had prayed to see God work like He had in the book of Acts. She was amazed how many people came to Christ in the first century and desired to see the Holy Spirit's power like wildfire in the hearts of the people in East Asia. When these older women arrived to help, she didn't expect much, but these women boldly shared the Gospel with anyone who would listen. Students flocked to the worker's apartment to hear these women they'd heard about. In less than five days, over 120 people came to Christ. A lesson of faith was learned as she watched an outpouring of the Holy Spirit among the people she had come to love.

You are equipped to be God's instrument because you have the Spirit's power. Never forget that! As you go into your office, your classroom, your neighborhood, huge foreign cities or into the jungle, God has equipped you, not with eloquence or superior wisdom but with something infinitely better. Even Paul was afraid, but that fear did not stop him from spreading the Good News. Do not let it stop you either. You may tremble as you witness. Just be sure to witness. The Spirit has empowered you just like He did these three short-term partners.

Lord, I thank You for enabling us to preach Your Word. Help us to tap into Your power as we spread Your Word. Give us courage. Give us Your words. And open the hearts of the people to receive Your Word and salvation. *In Jesus' name. Amen.*

RAISING SUPPORT

Read Exodus 25:1-2

"The LORD spoke to Moses: 'Tell the Israelites to take an offering for Me. You are to take My offering from everyone whose heart stirs him [to give].'"

For the second time around, Hunter wanted to go back to Africa on a mission trip. This time, her father and sister wanted to go with her, but since her dad had just lost his job, the finances for three members of their family to go seemed out of reach unless God intervened. Together, they prayed earnestly for God to provide what they could not earn themselves. One afternoon, a surprise gift of $500 arrived from a benefactor they didn't even know. That seemed to be the gift that God used to open the floodgates of support that came from family and friends. God showed His faithfulness to this family who desired to serve Him overseas.

Perhaps you want to go on a mission trip, but you don't have the money to go. This situation is common. Thank God that He prompts the hearts of His people to give! Pray that God will supply your needs. You may be surprised who God uses. We have received offerings for mission trip support from our dentist, unsaved friends and other believers who didn't have large bank accounts. God uses all kinds of people to support His work. Tell the Lord what you need and watch Him provide. At the same time, be careful to listen as He prompts your own heart.

Thank you, Father, for prompting our hearts to give. Father, I pray that You will abundantly bless each person who has given to this mission trip. And Father, I pray that You will continue to prompt people to give joyfully. Thank You for meeting our needs. *Amen.*

DAY EIGHT:

FORGIVENESS

Read Genesis 50:19-21

"'Therefore don't be afraid. I will take care of you and your little ones.'
And he comforted them and spoke kindly to them." (Genesis 50:21)

A Christian worker in Central Asia tells the story of Rose, a young national who became a believer while in college. When she told her father about her new faith, he beat her savagely and threw her out of the house. Three days later, she returned to the house to tell her father that she forgave him. Quite shocked by her response, he asked, "How do you do that after I beat you so badly?" She replied, "God has forgiven me. I must forgive you." Even though persecution from her family has continued, she is loving toward her undeserving parents.

There are many examples of biblical characters who completely forgave. Joseph's brothers were jealous of him because they thought their father favored him, so they sold him for 20 shekels of silver and told their father that their brother was dead. Many years later, the brothers are reunited and scared because their little brother has become a powerful man. Does Joseph punish them? Hardly. He speaks kindly and reassures them that he will provide for them and their children. Even though Joseph's brothers had wronged him, and apparently never sought to undo the harm they had done, Joseph responded with kindness and love.

What about you? Are you harboring unforgiveness in your heart? Has someone hurt you deeply? Maybe a church member, a trusted friend or a family member? Forgive them today and experience freedom.

Dear Father, thank You for forgiving me of my sin. I know that I do not deserve Your forgiveness, yet I receive it. Help me to forgive those who have wronged me so that I can be used for Your glory. *Amen.*

The Light of the World

Read Isaiah 9:2

"The people walking in darkness have seen a great light;
on those living in the land of darkness, a light has dawned."

While visiting a Buddhist temple in Southeast Asia, an uproar broke out with temple visitors who were angrily addressing our translators. They were furious that we had been brought to the temple because "their gods did not speak our language." We were thrilled to tell our translators that our God, the living God, indeed speaks their language. We watched as our translator Cassidy bowed to the god created by human hands. As the week progressed, however, Cassidy came to an understanding of what Jesus had done on the cross for her. When we returned to the temple at the end of the week, I gently told Cassidy that she could no longer bow to the created gods. With a huge smile, she responded, "I know. I am a Christian!"

Yes, it is the cry of our hearts for those walking in darkness to see the great Light! Jesus is the Light of the world. And so we go where God has called us—to our families, our neighbors, our co-workers and beyond. We go to countries and to people who are very different from us so that they will see our good works and glorify our Father who is in heaven (Matthew 5:16). Rejoice today that Jesus is the Light of the world (John 8:12), and let your light shine so that the world will glorify God!

Thank you, God, for saving us. Use us to bring life where there is death, light where there is darkness and peace where there is confusion.
We pray in Jesus' name. Amen.

Feet on the Path

Read Proverbs 4:25-27

"Let your eyes look forward;
fix your gaze straight ahead." (Proverbs 4:25)

As the team leader of the group, Harold was thrilled to be going to Colombia with 24 others from his church. One of their planned activities was door-to-door evangelism. The first day, Harold led nine people to the Lord.

But the next day, when he shared his faith through an interpreter to a mother and child, the woman immediately changed the subject to her disapproval of the United States "spreading war" around the world. Harold was shocked by her attacks on his country, and silently he prayed, "Dear God, please give me wisdom. Help me to stay focused on my real reason for being here." Although she was not interested in Christianity, Harold felt God's peace and was able to show her Christ's love and forgiveness.

God has called you to participate in missions. It is an honor and a privilege. Remember that the enemy will try to distract you. He will throw all kinds of things in your way, good or bad—anything to get your eyes unfocused. Keep your eyes on the joy of obedience and service to your Savior. When you find yourself distracted and swerving to the right or left, pray that God will keep your feet on the path. It is a great path to be on.

Father, thank You so much for putting my feet on this path! Please help me to look straight ahead. Keep my feet from evil. Help me to see distractions for what they are, and don't allow me to lose focus. I love You. Thank You for allowing me to serve You. *Amen.*

UNITY

Read John 17:6-19

"Holy Father, protect them by Your name that You have given Me, so that they may be one as We are one." (John 17:11b)

With a big smile, the new believer thanked me. As I spoke with her, I marveled at how many people God had used to bring this young woman to Him. Last summer, a team from Alabama prayerwalked the streets of Riobamba. Two weeks later, a team from Mississippi walked the same streets and distributed Gospel tracts. This woman received one of those tracts. After reading it, she called the phone number on the back and spoke to a local pastor. He and his wife visited her and led her to the Lord. A new Bible study soon began in her home. Who should receive the thanks that she expressed? The mission team members, the prayer and financial supporters, the national pastor and local church all played a part. All worked together to bring people into the kingdom.

Unity of believers is so important to Jesus. He prayed to His Father for us before He ascended into heaven. He asked God that we would be one, as He and His Father are one. Wow! Believe me when I tell you that the enemy will try to cause disunity among your team, with the missionary or with nationals. People can get on one another's nerves on a mission trip. Look for opportunities to serve your teammates and other partners. Obey your leaders, submit to others. You will be an answer to Jesus' prayer.

Father, we thank You that You have sent us into the world to speak Your truth. Make me a blessing to my teammates and to our partners. Give me a submissive and humble heart. Father, I pray that others will see how we love each other and they will be drawn to You. *Amen.*

Day Twelve:

Freedom for the Captives

Read Isaiah 61

"For as the earth brings forth its growth, and as a garden enables what is sown to spring up, so the Lord GOD will cause righteousness and praise to spring up before all the nations." (Isaiah 61:11)

Boris had been a prisoner of communism. He earnestly sought truth, but when he was told about Jesus, it was hard for him to believe because of his upbringing. We prayed for his salvation. Right before we were to leave his country, I asked him if he was a communist. He thought that I asked him if he was a Christian, and he responded that he wanted me to help him become one. Boris decided to follow Jesus that very day.

The Lord has anointed you to preach Good News to the poor, to build up the brokenhearted, to proclaim freedom to the captives and to release prisoners from darkness. There's no greater privilege. Read this chapter again while you are on your trip, and bask in the truth. God has chosen you to comfort those who mourn and to bring gladness instead of mourning. God is so good! He doesn't need us, but He chooses to work though us in a mighty way. Keep your eyes open for those who are hurting. Ask the Lord to reveal to you those who need His touch.

Lord, thank You that You have anointed me to preach Good News to the poor. Open my eyes to those who need Your healing. Use me to bring Your joy to all those with whom I have contact. My soul rejoices in You.

Amen.

WORSHIPPERS FROM EVERY NATION

Read Revelation 7:9-12

"After this I looked, and there was a vast multitude from every nation, tribe, people, and language, which no one could number, standing before the throne and before the Lamb." (Revelation 7:9a)

There is a traditional meal served in Central Asia called "five fingers." The meal is served on special occasions or for special guests in this Muslim culture. First, a lamb is slaughtered. Then the people prepare the mutton and serve the meat with noodles. Oh, how Muslims need the Lamb of God! For the Christian observing the special meal, the event is a reminder of what it means for a lamb to die. Jesus is the Lamb of God who was slain for the multitudes of people in the world, and one day, multitudes of believers of the Gospel from all different people groups will be around His throne.

I love this glimpse of heaven found in Revelation. Talk about diversity! Try to imagine this scene—people from every nation, tribe and language! We know that Jesus died for everyone, without exception. And yet we also know that there are many who have not heard. So we go with hearts burning with a passion for them to hear of Jesus who died for them. I believe one of the reasons God gave us this passage in Revelation was to encourage and motivate us to go. He is thrilled that you have answered that call to go on a mission trip. Praise God forever and ever!

Father, we look forward to the day when we will worship You with people from every nation, tribe and language. I pray that Your Gospel will be preached everywhere and that I would be a part of it. Worthy is the Lamb! *Amen.*

SALVATION

Read Romans 6:23

*"For the wages of sin is death, but the gift of God
is eternal life in Christ Jesus our Lord."*

As we walked the streets of Haiti telling the villagers of Christ's love, a group of children followed us. They don't usually see foreigners and were hoping for pieces of candy. After hearing the presentation of the Gospel numerous times, a little boy pulled on my shirt and told me that he wanted to receive Christ as his Savior. I reviewed the plan of salvation with him, and he assured me that he was ready to make this decision at home with his mother present. He led me to their tiny hut, and I explained to his mother about the child's desire. After hearing the Gospel, the mother also wanted to follow Christ. Mother and child together committed their lives to the Savior.

The whole message of salvation is found in this one verse in Romans. We are sinners who deserve death. God has given us the free gift of eternal life through Jesus Christ when we trust Him as our Lord and Savior. Be sure that you have received this gift of eternal life. If you have never done so before, pray to God. Tell Him that you know that you are a sinner in need of forgiveness. Tell Him that you believe that Jesus died for your sins and that He rose again. Ask Him to be your Savior. Tell Him that you want Him to be Lord of your life. If you already have received Christ as your Savior, be prepared to tell others how they too can be saved. Consider memorizing Romans 6:23.

Father, thank You for the gift of salvation through Christ Jesus. Help me to share this Good News with others.

Amen.

THE GREAT COMMISSION

Read Matthew 28:19-20

"Go, therefore, and make disciples of all nations, baptizing them in the name of the Father and of the Son and of the Holy Spirit, teaching them to observe everything I have commanded you. And remember, I am with you always, to the end of the age."

We brought a team of nurses to the Dominican Republic to conduct medical clinics. While we were walking along a village street, a woman beckoned for us to come to her house. She was suffering from a terrible headache and said that she had dreamed we would come. Dona, our nurse, was able to give her medication to relieve her headache. While we were there, her brother-in-law came home. We shared the Gospel with him, and he trusted Christ as his Savior.

Jesus told us to go. We go with joy and sometimes with fear and trembling. Jesus loves the whole world, and He wants them to know how much He loves them. He has entrusted us with the responsibility of spreading the Gospel. But He does not send us alone. He promises that He is with us always. What a comfort and a blessing!

Lord, we thank You for this tremendous responsibility. Enable us to go and make disciples through Your power. We thank You that You are always with us.

Amen.

How Can They Hear?

Read Romans 10:11-15

*"But how can they call on Him in whom they have not believed?
And how can they believe without hearing about Him?
And how can they hear without a preacher?" (Romans 10:14)*

God placed in our hearts a vision to bring sight, both physical and spiritual, to the village of Bois de Lance, Haiti. With hearts full of anticipation and suitcases full of eyeglasses, our team boarded the plane. After examining each patient who came to the clinic and fitting each one with a pair of glasses, a counselor shared the Gospel of Christ and waited for a response.

One morning, we were informed that a man who was lingering around the clinic was a witch doctor. We all prayed that he would come to the clinic and hear the Good News of salvation. Later in the day, God answered our prayers. When confronted with the Gospel, he told his counselor that he was involved in voodoo and therefore could "not go up." The counselor assured him that Christ had died for him and desired for him to go to heaven. The witch doctor bowed his head and prayed to receive Jesus as his Savior and Lord. He then proclaimed, "No more voodoo!"

Everyone who calls on the name of the Lord will be saved. I believe this with all of my heart. But Paul asks us how they can hear without someone preaching to them. Most of us were blessed to live our lives where the Good News of Jesus is everywhere. If we want to know about the Bible, it is easy for us to find out. However, there are people all over the world who have never heard about Jesus. God has chosen you to go and tell them.

Father, we don't know why You have chosen to work through us, but we are grateful. Prepare us now for the work You have for us to do. Thank You.

Amen.

DAY SEVENTEEN:

SEND ME!

Read Isaiah 6:1-8

"Then I heard the voice of the Lord saying: Who should I send? Who will go for Us? I said: Here I am. Send me." (Isaiah 6:8)

While in Africa as a student short-term missions partner, April was discouraged about her inadequacy. Satan had convinced her that she was of no help to the people of Malawi. "Can God really make lifelong changes in these people's lives through our team?" she wondered. That's when she felt God telling her, "April, I created them, and I will take care of them. Let go and trust Me. You did your part by obeying the call to go. That is all I ask of you. Well done." Relieved, she put her faith in God that He was the one who changed people, not her.

Sometimes we think we can't be ambassadors for Christ because we're not good enough. Our enemy, the accuser, reminds us of all the rotten things we've said and done, and we begin to feel defeated. We think about how unworthy we are and question our ability to go and preach. This passage in Isaiah describes how I often see myself for who I really am, a filthy sinner. Isaiah said, "Woe is me, for I am ruined, because I am a man of unclean lips and live among a people of unclean lips." Sounds like the 21st century! And yet, Isaiah's response to this exclamation was not to sit at home and sulk but to offer himself to the Lord. The angel told him that his guilt was taken away, and he immediately volunteered his life to God. As a way to show gratitude, we can go and tell others, too.

Thank you, Father, for saving us. We know that we are unworthy. Thank You for sending us to tell others of Your love and grace.

Amen.

Be Alert

Read 1 Peter 5:8-9

"Be sober! Be on the alert! Your adversary the Devil is prowling around like a roaring lion, looking for anyone he can devour." (1 Peter 5:8)

Four New Mexican short-term partners came to work alongside a missionary and Russian pastor for a week in the Republic of Bashkortostan, ministering in an orphanage, an agricultural institute and through evangelistic events. But from the very beginning, the local government authorities dedicated themselves to squashing that plan. One by one, cancellations came, often just hours before the planned event. As a result of closed doors, the team went to the local church to discuss the situation. It seemed like the local authorities had won. But God brought two young women to the church while the team wondered what God had in mind. They were able to tell the women about God's love and about salvation through faith in Christ. The missionary then shared his salvation story. God, not the government authorities, was glorified that day.

God tells us to be alert. We have an enemy who wants to devour us. If you are feeling discouraged or confused and afraid, the enemy is attacking you. He doesn't want you to undertake this work. He wants you complacent and defeated. Don't be surprised when you are attacked. You are a soldier in God's kingdom. Satan would delight in seeing you give up on this mission. Remember that God is more powerful than the enemy. Stand firm. Rejoice in the victory that is sure.

Father, we thank You for the victory we have in You. Help us to be strong and steadfast in You. We love You.

Amen.

CREATED FOR A PURPOSE

Read Ephesians 2:1-10

"For we are His creation—created in Christ Jesus for good works, which God prepared ahead of time so that we should walk in them." (Ephesians 2:10)

For years, Janie had been saving money for a down payment on a house. The cost of an upcoming mission trip was almost the same amount as what she had saved. But Janie knew that God wanted her to go. She opened her Bible, and it fell open to Matthew 19:29-30: "And everyone who has left houses, brothers or sisters, father or mother, children, or fields because of My name will receive 100 times more …" Those verses spoke to Janie, and she decided to trust God with her down payment. After the mission trip to Romania, her life was changed. She contacted a mission agency to see if she could go for an extended time and was accepted to serve in the Middle East for nine months. When the term was over, she returned to the States to find that her 401K had more than doubled, giving her more than enough for a down payment on a house. She was fulfilling God's purpose for her life, and He chose to bless her.

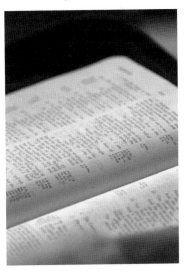

You were created to do good works, just like Janie. Not just any good works but those prepared in advance for you by God. Now you are preparing for a mission trip. You may be saving money, collecting shoes, packing your tools or studying the Bible. As you feed the poor, care for the sick or teach Vacation Bible School, remember that God planned your deeds. It is not by accident that you will make a difference. You were created to give God glory.

Lord, thank You for preparing good works for us to do. We can't wait to see the work You have for us. We are excited to serve You. You are amazing! *Amen.*

Day Twenty:

Peace of God

Read Philippians 4:4-13

"And the peace of God, which surpasses every thought,
will guard your hearts and your minds in Christ Jesus." (Philippians 4:7)

We were on our way to the Indian reservation and stopped to fill our tanks with gas. I had taken a group of girls to the restroom when I heard someone yell, "Audie was run over!" We ran to see what had happened and discovered Audie on the ground. He had indeed been run over by a car, not once, but twice. The driver had backed the car over his leg and then driven forward over the same leg. There were tire tracks on his pants, but his leg was unharmed! The only explanation was that God had protected him.

As you prepare for your mission trip, many concerns may come to your mind. Will my family be OK without me? What about my job? How will I pay for this? What if I get sick? Will there be plumbing? How will I communicate? There are so many unknowns, and sometimes we fear the unknown. God's Word tells us not to be anxious but to present our requests to Him with thanksgiving. God will take care of our families, our finances, our health and all our needs. Tell the Lord your concerns. He will trade them for peace.

Father, You know the situations I am facing. You know far more about it than I do. Thank You for taking care of me. You are a great God and loving Father. Help me to rest in You.
Amen.

FASTING

Read Isaiah 58:6-14

"Isn't the fast I choose: To break the chains of wickedness, to untie the ropes of the yoke, to set the oppressed free, and to tear off every yoke?" (Isaiah 58:6)

After 9/11, we took a team to the Middle East. We decided to begin by fasting and prayerwalking in a particular city. As a group, we prayed as we walked the streets, and eventually we met a young boy and asked him if we could pray for him. As we talked, he came to understand his need for a Savior and accepted Christ.

Before we went on this trip, God directed me to Mark 16:15-18: "Then He said to them, 'Go into all the world and preach the gospel to the whole creation. Whoever believes and is baptized will be saved, but whoever does not believe will be condemned. And these signs will accompany those who believe: In My name they will drive out demons; they will speak in new languages; they will pick up snakes; if they should drink anything deadly, it will never harm them; they will lay hands on the sick, and they will get well." Walking the streets, we surveyed the lostness. Our hearts ached for the women hidden behind veils and the men who spoke angrily to them if they reached for the New Testaments offered. One man even put a live snake in the faces of Michael and Rochelle, two team members, when they offered him a copy of God's Word. And indeed, the snake did not hurt them.

Fasting is the discipline of going without food for a period of time as you concentrate on prayer. It is powerful. Consider a day of fasting before your mission trip. Maybe you can fast a meal or even for a 24-hour period. Maybe your whole team would be willing to pick a meal or a day to dedicate to prayer and fasting. It will not be easy, but I think you will be blessed.

Father, we thank You for who You are and what You have done. We humble ourselves before You. We are Your servants. Show us Your will. *We pray in Jesus' name. Amen.*

Day Twenty-two:

Celebration

Read Nehemiah 8

"Ezra blessed the LORD, the great God, and with their hands uplifted all the people said, 'Amen, Amen!' Then they bowed down and worshiped the LORD with their faces to the ground." (Nehemiah 8:6)

Two mission teams of Brazilians and Americans came to one of the least evangelized cities in Brazil in order to visit 500 homes of mostly nonbelievers. One particular home was comprised of a father, mother and teenage son.

Twice before, the son had tried to commit suicide, so the parents were desperate for any encouragement. On the day of the visit, the teams received word that the son had been rushed to the hospital after his third suicide attempt. After praying for a chance to meet the son, one of the short-term partners, a Brazilian pastor's wife and a missionary couple were able to share Jesus with this young man in the presence of his parents. Not only did the son accept Christ, but the father and mother did also. A few weeks later after conducting a Bible study in their home, the mother said, "Thank you not just for helping us understand the Bible better but for sharing the Good News that saved our family."

You will have many opportunities to celebrate and see God at work on your mission trip, just like these teams. In Nehemiah, the Israelites celebrated in a seven-day feast. Their joy was great. We also can delight in and worship God for who He is and what He has done for us. Our joy is important to the Lord, and we have so much to be happy about, especially our salvation.

Father, we praise Your holy and precious name. Thank You for sending us. We rejoice in who You are and who we are in You.

In Jesus' name. Amen.

SILENT VOICE

Read Psalm 19

"There is no speech; there are no words;
their voice is not heard." (Psalm 19:3)

Trekking through the Himalayas with a missionary and two Buddhist porters, Beth couldn't believe the beauty that she saw and experienced. As a student summer missionary, she rejoiced in the breathtaking views as their team traveled to numerous remote villages to share the Gospel. The porters showed an interest in the "Good Book" as they spent time together, so they were given Bibles. After two weeks, they asked how one follows Jesus. The team and Beth were so excited when these two became their brothers in Christ. "Everyone could see the love of the Lord on their faces," said Beth. God was glorified as He drew these men to the Creator, the One they had always wondered about in their deepest thoughts.

We go in Jesus' name, declaring the glory of God. We go with joy. It is our privilege to tell others of our God who has saved us. However, before we speak and before anyone has spoken of God's works, the heavens have declared the glory of God. The skies and mountains have proclaimed the work of His hand. God has proclaimed His greatness by His handiwork to the very ends of the earth. As we speak of our God to the world, they have already seen and experienced God's glory as they looked at nature. God is not hidden. His glory is manifest everywhere.

Thank you, Father, for revealing Yourself to us through what You created. Help us to always be looking for You in all things. Continue to reveal Yourself to us and through us. *Amen.*

Bread from Heaven

Read Exodus 16:1-4

*"Then the LORD said to Moses,
'I am going to rain bread from heaven for you …'"* (Exodus 16:4a)

A young man asking for prayer approached a mission team visiting Thailand. Bonnie, one of the team members, learned that he requested prayer concerning the intense persecution he received due to his conversion to Christianity. He had been robbed and beaten. He had been disowned by his family and lived alone. Specifically, he did not ask for protection or for relief from the trials, but the young man only asked the team to pray that he would be strong enough to respond to his persecutors with love. Bonnie was astounded and thought of the many times that she had complained to God about her own trials while asking God to remove them, not wanting to face the lack of love in her own heart. She was forever impacted by this Thai Christian, and this man was encouraged in his faith that day as others prayed for him.

Perhaps we can all relate to the Israelites when they were slaves in Egypt, living a miserable existence. God sent Moses to deliver them, remember? He parted the Red Sea for them so they could walk to freedom and then closed the sea to devour their enemies. It was a marvelous, miraculous provision. And then they complained that they missed the food they had in Egypt and wished to return to captivity. God rescued them so lovingly, and they responded with complaints. How did God respond to their complaints about the food? He rained down bread from heaven for them. I am continually amazed at God's goodness and grace. He showers us with undeserved blessings day after day.

Father, I know that I often complain and am ungrateful for all You have done for me. Forgive me, Father. Thank You for Your blessings that abound in my life. Thank You for the example of this Thai believer who did not complain. I love You. *Amen.*

Prayer Partners

Read 2 Corinthians 1:10-11

"He has delivered us from such a terrible death, and He will deliver us; we have placed our hope in Him that He will deliver us again. And you can join in helping with prayer for us, so that thanks may be given by many on our behalf for the gift that came to us through [the prayers of] many."

D.H. was nearly 8 years old when her parents took her to the rescue mission run by the Campbells. It was on the "other side of town," a place that was dramatically different from what she knew. The people coming to the mission truly needed to be rescued. As the years went by, D.H.'s mom insisted that they visit Mrs. Campbell, but as a teenager, she dreaded the visits. Life went on for D.H. as she graduated from college, did a two-year missionary term, got married and then became a career missionary. During all her missionary years, D.H. received letter after letter from Mrs. Campbell. Although she was practically blind, the elderly woman wrote each letter with a magnifying machine. D.H. learned that this precious woman not only was a prayer warrior for her but also for many missionaries. She made it a point to visit Mrs. Campbell when she was in the States. When Mrs. Campbell died, D.H. thanked God for this hero of the faith who spent time on her knees for God's work to be accomplished.

Never underestimate the power of prayer! You are praying as you prepare for your trip. Be sure to ask others to pray with you and for you, now and while you are away. Your prayer partners are a vital part of the mission team. Let them know of your needs, joys and challenges. Their role is of paramount importance.

Father, Thank You that You listen to our prayers and that You answer them. Reveal to me the names of people who will join our team in prayer. Thank You for providing people who are willing to pray for us.

Amen.

Day Twenty-six:

God's Word Speaks

Read Isaiah 55:6-13

"… My word that comes from My mouth will not return to Me empty,
but it will accomplish what I please, and will prosper
in what I send it [to do]." (Isaiah 55:11)

Sharing with complete strangers in a country in South America was out of Sara's comfort zone, but it was evident that the Lord had been preparing this mission team member. "It wasn't difficult to talk about the Lord working in my life or to explain salvation," said Sara, "but remembering Scripture to back up my beliefs was new to me. The Lord showed me that my words are nothing, but His Word is the most powerful tool for witnessing." One hot afternoon, Sara talked with a mother and her two teenagers. She used God's Word to explain how Jesus died on the cross for them as they listened intently. Sara exclaimed, "I felt tears as I shared the excitement of serving a living God."

God sends us out with joy and leads us in peace. Sometimes it seems our words fall on deaf ears, but God assures us of something different. He tells us that His Word will not return empty but will accomplish His purposes. What comfort this promise brings! We may not always see the fruit of our labor, but we can be confident that God will complete His work. Our only job is to be obedient. God's ways are so much higher than ours. We praise Him for His words and His ways.

Thank You, Father, for this passage in Isaiah. Help us to speak Your Word, believing it will accomplish all You have planned.
We pray in Jesus' name. Amen.

Day Twenty-seven:

Beautiful Feet

Read Isaiah 52:7-12

"How beautiful on the mountains are the feet of the herald, who proclaims peace, who brings news of good things, who proclaims salvation, who says to Zion, 'Your God reigns!'" (Isaiah 52:7)

"We've heard about Jesus, but now we have seen Jesus in these men," said the headman in the Kakomba area of Zambia. He was speaking of three missions partners, Byron, Mike and Damian, who had worked tirelessly at a weekend campaign for Christ. As a result, a new church was born. Each year, many Christians in local churches pay their own way to serve the Lord for a short time in a place far from home. It does take a lot of money and energy, but they go to show people Jesus.

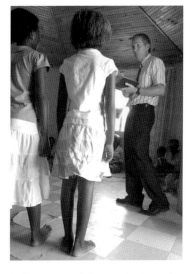

Isaiah 52:10b says that "all the ends of the earth will see the salvation of our God." And the Lord talks about those who bring Good News—you. You are going to proclaim peace and salvation. God says your feet are beautiful! You may have never thought about your feet being lovely, but God sees you as a beautiful messenger of His love and grace. In this same passage, we learn that the Lord will go before us, and the God of Israel will be our rear guard. We are well protected.

Thank You, Father, for protecting us, for going before us and behind us. We do shout with joy because You have redeemed us. Thank You for sending us to proclaim peace and salvation. *In Jesus' name. Amen.*

PRAYER ACTION

Read Matthew 6:9-13

"Therefore, you should pray like this …" *(Matthew 6:9)*

The Navajo reservation was dry and barren. At 120 degrees, it was so hot, it seemed difficult to breathe. Water was the most precious commodity. Except for the few Christians who had tasted Living Water, the hearts of the people were as parched as their land. They worshipped the created rather than the Creator. Our team rose early with the sun to worship the Lord together in song, prayer and Bible study before retreating for private quiet time to seek the Lord. On this particular morning, I praised the Lord for the beauty of His creation and prayed for Him to use me to reach the lost. As I walked back to the compound, I came upon a young boy sitting alone on the sand. His father was a tribal leader, a priest of their false religion. As I shared the Gospel with him, he quietly bowed his head and turned his life over to God.

Prayer is where we have to start in ministry, but how do we pray? The acronym ACTS has been used to help us remember how Jesus taught the disciples to pray. "A" is for adoration. It is important for us to come to God, adoring Him for who He is. Jesus said, "Hallowed be Your name." (KJV) As we adore God, our spirit is in tune with His. "C" is for confession. We confess our sins to God so that we can also be forgiven. "T" is for thanksgiving. We have much to be thankful for, beginning with salvation. And finally "S" is for supplication, making our requests to God. "Don't worry about anything, but in everything, through prayer and petition with thanksgiving, let your requests be made known to God." (Philippians 4:6) Prayer is an awesome privilege. "Pray constantly." (1 Thessalonians 5:17)

Father, we adore You. We confess our sins, knowing we are not worthy of Your love. We thank You for Jesus who died for us. Thank You for allowing us to serve You on this mission team. Bless us and provide for us. Use us for Your glory. *Amen.*

COMPLETING THE WORK

Read Philippians 1:3-6

"I am sure of this, that He who started a good work in you will carry it on to completion until the day of Christ Jesus." (Philippians 1:6)

We were walking from hut to hut in the small Haitian village, talking to people about the love of Jesus. We spoke to Wanelle of Jesus' love, and he gave us a familiar refrain: "I want to accept Christ, but I am not ready." I said, "Today is the day of salvation. We don't know that we will have tomorrow." He responded by telling us that he would receive Christ if we came back tomorrow at the same time. The next day, we returned to the hut promptly. We resolved to be faithful, despite the unlikelihood of reaping a harvest. As expected, Wanelle was nowhere to be found when we arrived, but we asked for him. After a few short minutes, he arrived. I immediately got to the point and reminded him of his promise. He then removed his hat and dropped to his knees.

God starts a work in us, and sometimes it seems to stall out. Has that ever happened to you? Are you experiencing that now? You felt sure God wants you to be a part of this mission team and perhaps now you're not so sure. Maybe you see obstacles everywhere you look. Now is the time to look up to your Provider, not at your circumstances. God promises that He will be faithful to complete the work that He has begun in you. So pray with joy, and see what God will do!

Thank you, God, that You always complete what You start. You are always faithful. Your mercies are new every morning. Please help me to be faithful to You and the work that You have called me to do.

Amen.

Work Together

Read 1 Corinthians 3:6

"I planted, Apollos watered, but God gave the growth."

When Tom arrived in East Asia with his church mission team, he thought that he would be helping with an annual missionary meeting. But when a team member asked him if he was willing to do anything, Tom heartily replied, "Yes!" So instead of joining his wife and others leading Bible study for missionary kids, he found himself in charge of food distribution and mail delivery at a refugee camp. There he saw people displaced by murder and war coming to Christ. He could have been disappointed because of the change of plans. "Even though situations may stretch us," said Tom, "we will find great worth in doing God's will without wavering."

Mission team members have many roles, but together they make up a team. You may be the captain or the water boy. Neither is more important than the other. This passage in 1 Corinthians tells us that we all have one purpose, and we will each be rewarded according to our labor. Because of our sinful nature, it is tempting to look at others and wonder why they hold certain positions or get to do certain jobs. Miriam wondered why her brother, Moses, got the better job, and even the disciples asked, "What about him?" It is only God who gives life and sustains it. Don't waste time and energy looking at others with envy. Don't compete with your teammates. Serve with a happy heart.

Thank You, God, that we are your fellow workers. Help me to work only to please You. I confess that I am sometimes jealous of others. Forgive me. Help me to serve You and only You with my whole heart. *Amen.*

DAY THIRTY-ONE:

NAMES OF GOD

Read Revelation 1:4-8

"For a child will be born for us, a son will be given to us, and the government will be on His shoulders. He will be named Wonderful Counselor, Mighty God, Eternal Father, Prince of Peace." (Isaiah 9:6)

We arrived in Haiti to conduct an eye clinic. Our team had been preparing for months, and we felt prepared to do the work God called us to do. The day we arrived, the national pastor informed us that in addition to the eye clinic, he wanted us to conduct a Vacation Bible School. The VBS was to last from 8 a.m. to 3 p.m., and he was expecting 250 children. With no materials or preparation, we knew our God would have to give us all that we needed. We greeted the children in the morning with smiles on our faces and trembling in our hearts. We taught them every song we'd ever heard and played every game we knew. And we told them about Jesus. When we gave an opportunity for the children to respond, 39 children wanted to follow Christ. Our Lord is Jehovah-Jireh, the God who provides.

The Bible is full of many names for God. Elohim means total power and might. El Elyon means God, Most High. Adonai means Lord, master or owner. As you worship God today, speak His names. Thank Him that He is El Roi—the God who sees. Praise Him that He is the God who provides, the Alpha and Omega, the beginning and the end. As we speak the names of God, we get a glimpse of who He is. This brings us peace, comfort and joy.

God, I thank You for who You are. You are my Lord and Savior. You are the Prince of Peace. I love You, Lord. Bless this mission trip, and thank You for what You have taught me this past month. *Amen.*

MONTH-TO-MONTH CHECKLIST
FOR MISSION TRIP TEAMS[1]

10-12 Months Prior to Departure:
– Select a team leader
– Research available assignments
– Accept assignment
– Begin publicity of mission trip

6 Months Prior:
– Meet with prospective team members
– Recruit prayer team
– Study country or area information
– Find out what official documents are required to enter the country
– Contact travel agency concerning transportation and lodging
– Find out what inoculations are needed and the time frame required for them
– Send a proposed copy of the itinerary to field personnel who will verify that this time is appropriate
– Complete and submit required forms for participating
– Establish a budget for the trip
– Establish a per person cost

5 Months Prior:
– Team members should fill out applications, medical questionnaires, international travel release forms and other important documents required so that the team leader or committee can begin selection process

4 Months Prior:
– Team members should apply for passports
– Order training materials for trip
– Have informational meeting
– Announce training schedule

3 Months Prior:
– Collect nonrefundable deposit from team members
– Collect photocopy of passport photo and vital information
– Get required inoculations
– Purchase tickets from travel agent and go over ground transportation plans
– Begin a prayer journal

10 Weeks Prior:
– Mail out support letters—have fundraisers
– Collect passports to apply for visas (may need more time for this)
– Enlist prayer partners

8 Weeks Prior:
– Work with field personnel on final plans
– Confirm all plans with travel agent
– Team members should prepare and practice their testimony

6 Weeks Prior:
– Team members should give all emergency contact information to team leader
– Team members should have appropriate emergency medical insurance
– Plan for special medical requirements
– Make team roster with addresses and phone numbers
– Have a practice prayerwalk

4 Weeks Prior:
– Confirm no less than 10 prayer partners per team member
– Team members should know their responsibilities
– Make second payments
– Start Get Set devotional

3 Weeks Prior:
– Discuss packing list and packing tips
– Collect all remaining forms
– Discuss team members' finances
– Break in any new shoes for the trip to avoid blisters
– Obtain either cash or traveler's checks for departure
– Prepare a team medical kit
– Share your itinerary with prayer partners
– Organize an e-mail prayer chain for during the trip
– Call your cell phone carrier to enroll in an overseas plan (usually inexpensive)

2 Weeks Prior:
– Discuss journaling
– Get final update on team finances
– Double-check that all visas, passports and other documents are in order
– Schedule post-trip follow-up meetings
– Schedule post-trip team presentation to home church
– Make arrangements for transportation to and from home airport
– Purchase all supplies for trip

1 Week Prior:
– Pack and check luggage weight
– Tie matching ribbons around the handles of all team members' luggage
– Pack a change of clothes in your carry-on
– Pack each day's clothing in a large zip-lock type bag (keeps clothes organized and clean)
– Pack a few snacks
– Pack a copy of your passport and a copy of your insurance plan in a place different from the originals
– Notify your credit card company/bank of the dates you will be overseas so that charges will be honored
– Inform team members when and where to meet at airport
– Collect final payments
– Give team members a list of emergency numbers for team
– Distribute any items team members need to pack
– Individuals should collect cash or traveler's checks if needed for personal use
– Team should be commissioned
– Confirm all details with travel agent one last time

During trip:
– Journal your insights

After trip:
– Express gratitude to your financial and prayer partners
– Report back to your church
– Express appreciation to field personnel
– Consider another mission trip

[1]Sinquefield, Danny. Team Leader Training (Richmond, Va.: The International Mission Board, 2007), pp. 173-177.

· Resources

Missions Opportunities and Preparation Web Sites:
Beautiful Feet International: **beautifulfeetinternational.net**
IMB: **going.imb.org/volunteers**

Team Training:
Basic Training for Mission Teams (DVD/CD/Workbook)—available at
imbresources.org and **Lifeway.com**

My Life His Mission (6-week study for student mission teams)—available at
imbresources.org or call 1-800-999-3113

Preach and Heal (resource for medical mission teams)—available at
imbresources.org or call 1-800-999-3113

Team Leader Training (Manual for Team Leaders)—available from IMB.
Call **1-800-999-3113**, option **3**

Safe Travel Solutions (DVD training to keep your team secure overseas)—
available at **safetravelsolutions.org** or call 1-866-289-5505

Successful Mission Teams: A Guide for Volunteers. Rev. ed. by Martha
VanCise, Birmingham, AL; New Hope Publishers

Prayerwalking Resources:
Follow Me: Becoming a Lifestyle Prayerwalker (6-week study for the beginning
prayerwalker) available at **imbresources.org** or call 1-800-999-3113, option 3

Prayerwalking, Praying On Site With Insight (book) available at
imbresources.org or call **1-800-999-3113**

Immunizations, insurance, passports, visas, etc—see
going.imb.org/volunteers

Research:
IMB Global Research: **imb.org/globalresearch**
Peoplegroups.org: **peoplegroups.org**
Joshua Project: **joshuaproject.net**
Ethnologue: **ethnologue.com**
CIA World Factbook: **cia.gov/library/publications/the-world-factbook**

Additional Copies of *Get Set* are available at **imbresources.org** or call **1-800-
999-3113**, option **3.**